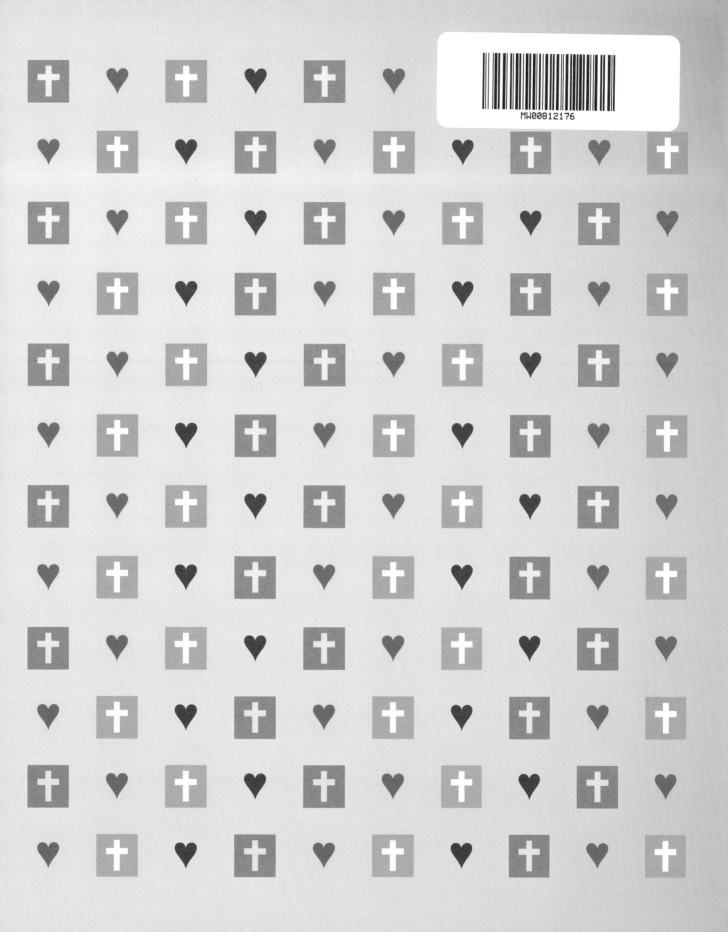

This book belongs to

_____

First edition 2021
This edition published 2022 by Ascension Publishing Group, LLC

Copyright © 2021 Anno Domini Publishing
www.ad-publishing.co.uk
Text copyright © 2021 Suzy Senior
Illustrations copyright © 2021 Dubravka Kolanovic

Publishing Director: Annette Reynolds
Art Director: Gerald Rogers
Pre-production: GingerPromo, Kev Holt

Editorial review for Ascension by Amy Welborn

Ascension
PO Box 1990
West Chester, PA 19380
www.ascensionpress.com
1-800-376-0520

ISBN 978-1-954881-42-6

Printed in the
United States of America

21 22 23 24 25 26 5 4 3 2 1

BASED ON THE PARABLE OF THE PHARISEE AND THE TAX COLLECTOR

The Bear that Nobody Wanted

Written by
Sally Ann Wright

Illustrated by
Krisztina Kállai Nagy

ASCENSION
Kids
West Chester, PA

Lion was sending out invitations.
Everyone was invited to his home—
every creature from every corner
of the world.

"Even Bear?" said Hawk.

"Everyone!" said Lion.

"But they will have to cross the fast-
flowing river," said Hawk.

"I will send everyone a pair of boots,"
said Lion. "Then everyone can come,
whoever they are."

The day came when all the creatures from every corner of the world were invited to Lion's home. Lion was very excited. Even Hawk was excited. Many had replied to the invitation and said they were coming.

"But I hope even more will come today," said Lion.

Lion went down to the fast-flowing river. He planned to step into the water himself to help everyone cross to the other side. He could already see them coming, all sorts of animals, all wearing the boots he had sent them.

Lion stepped into the water, which flowed around his furry legs.

He helped Zebra and Giraffe, Chicken and Dove. He helped Badger, Duck and Dodo, Goat and Owl, Rhino and Ring-Tailed Lemur, Deer and Wolf. He helped tiny Shrew and slow, slow Tortoise. That took a while.

They were all wearing the boots he had sent them and gathered on the other side of the fast-flowing river.

9

Lion helped Racoon, Sheep and Hippo, Kangaroo and Koala, Horse and Tiger, Rabbit, who had a damaged ear, Cow, Meerkat and Pig. He helped bad-tempered Alligator, Antelope, and even Penguin and two shy, pink Flamingos.

They were all wearing the boots he had sent them and gathered on the other side of the fast-flowing river.

Lion helped sleepy Dormouse and Fox, who had a poorly leg, mischievous Monkey, Cheetah and Toucan. He helped lumbering Elephant and elegant Reindeer.

They were all wearing the boots he had sent them and gathered on the other side of the fast-flowing river.

Lion smiled at each one who had made the journey and thanked them for coming. "Welcome to my home," he said.

There were some more creatures a few paces off but none of them had answered Lion's invitation.

Lion could see Bear, sitting
on a rock and looking
down at his boots.

"Don't those boots look silly?" said Peacock. "I didn't bring mine. I am sure I don't need them, and I don't want to spoil the way I look.

"I always look just right for every occasion."

"I didn't bring mine, either," said Squirrel.
"I couldn't carry them as well as all these nuts."

"Oh, how clever of you to bring nuts," said Peacock.
"May I share them?"

"Well, no," said Squirrel, struggling to keep hold of the
huge number he had brought. "I might not have enough for
later—I never share my nuts!"

"Never share?" said Cat.
"I ALWAYS share. In fact, I give
away so much of everything I
have that I barely have enough
for me…

18

"I am SO generous that I even gave away the boots Lion sent me (they weren't really my style anyway). I am ALWAYS doing things for others.

"But look! Who's that? Surely not… Bear! Why is he here? Nobody wants Bear!"

Squirrel and Peacock and Cat
all stared at Bear.

"Why are you here?"
they asked.

"Surely Lion didn't invite you!" said Peacock. "You are shabby and dirty… and look silly in those boots. Nobody wants Bear!"

"You are poor and ragged and have nothing to offer anyone," said Squirrel. "I don't know why you came. Nobody wants Bear!"

"You are not kind or generous," said Cat. "You don't help other people. You have never done a kind thing in your life! Nobody wants Bear!"

Bear continued to hang his head and stare at his boots.

"You are right," Bear said at last. "I am dirty and shabby. These boots are the only nice thing I have. I have never been kind or generous. But Lion was so generous to give me these boots, that I want to change and be kind like him."

Cat turned away, "Lion doesn't want you," she said.

Just then they all heard Lion calling them.

"Welcome," Lion called to Peacock, to Squirrel, to Cat, and to Bear. "Come and I will help you cross the fast-flowing river."

Peacock, Squirrel, and Cat looked at Bear and then looked at each other... and then they turned away to make the journey back to where they came from.

"Welcome," Lion called again to Bear. "Come and I will help you cross the fast-flowing river."

Bear looked at Lion's kind, smiling face. He reached out and took Lion's hand. He walked through the fast-flowing river in the boots that Lion had given him—and joined the others in Lion's home.

THE PARABLE OF THE PHARISEE AND THE TAX COLLECTOR

He also told this parable to some who trusted in themselves that they were righteous and despised others: "Two men went up into the temple to pray, one a Pharisee and the other a tax collector. The Pharisee stood and prayed thus with himself, 'God, I thank you that I am not like other men, extortioners, unjust, adulterers, or even like this tax collector. I fast twice a week, I give tithes of all that I get.'

But the tax collector, standing far off, would not even lift up his eyes to heaven, but beat his breast, saying, 'God, be merciful to me a sinner!' I tell you, this man went down to his house justified rather than the other; for every one who exalts himself will be humbled, but he who humbles himself will be exalted."

–Luke 18:9–14

29

This book is based on a story that Jesus told. God invites us all to be his friends and helps us find our way to him. We have to be humble enough to know we need his help and say yes.

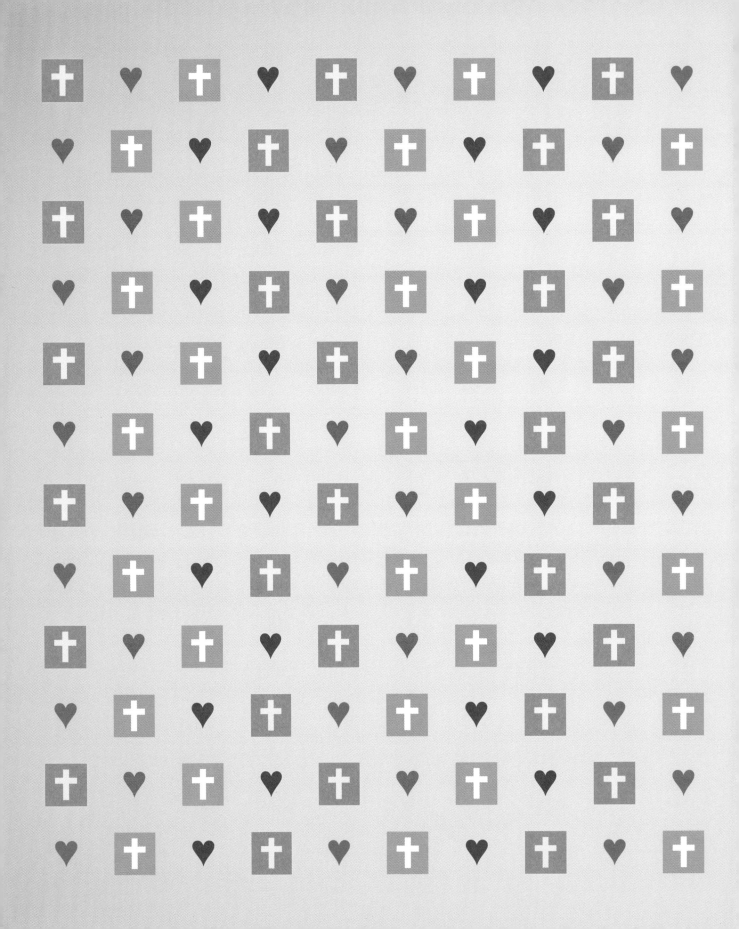